I0621271

The Path to Emotional Greatness: Yielding to Personal Transformation (EGYPT)

The Trinity Strategy Guidebook

by

Kenya Lee
RN, BSN, PHN

Fig Tree Publishing
USA

The Path to Emotional Greatness: Yielding to Personal Transformation (EGYPT): The Trinity Strategy Guidebook
Copyright © 2022 by Kenya Lee

Cover Art by Dawn Til Dusk Designs Copyright© 2022

Cover photo by Eugene Tkachenko Copyright © 2022

ISBN: 979-8-9866905-3-7—paperback
979-8-9866905-1-3—hardback

Fig Tree Publishing

Introduction

Kenya Lee is a registered nurse, social activist, artist, and writer. She grew up in Detroit, Michigan, where the struggles of urban childhood and adolescence fueled her passion for helping young women succeed in life. Her life journey to evolve into emotional wellness was preceded by hardships that threatened her very ability to succeed in life. Kenya has documented her path with the help of her eighteen years of memoirs that were primarily written during those times of heartache and struggle. This very practical book details her journey and sheds light on emotional transformation. It offers three proven strategies to reach emotional wellness as well as desired life goals.

Kenya founded Faith In Girls, Inc., in 2012 for the purpose of providing insight for young women while transitioning into adulthood. The organization operates on the philosophy that life can be challenging. However, the change in emotional awareness creates opportunity for any woman to succeed. Issues can arise, but education and awareness of self is the key to a less turbulent transition into womanhood. FIG provides interactive workshops in various community centers and virtual settings. The use of art and self-expression are used to provide the framework for the emotional shift needed to attain emotional clarity.

This book is designed with the intent of giving women coping skills for common life encounters. The book provides easy to understand tools that can be utilized throughout life, enhancing the element of positivity while encountering difficult life events and social influences. The Trinity Strategy was developed by Kenya and has helped countless women attain emotional greatness while yielding to their personal transformation.

Dedication

To my husband Joey, my biggest fan and my greatest supporter of my mission and vision. Thank you for your understanding of my journey and the woman I've become.

To my greatest life manifestation Ms. Egypt Nile, thank you for pure bliss and your innocent wisdom. This book is dedicated to your pure embodiment of consciousness. Thank you for coming.

-Always Accept the Challenge

The Journey Begins

Explaining to a person that is setting out to walk from North America to the Middle East with only their legs and feet with no motor transportation in the 21st century seems like an impossible task and an even more impossible thought. My arrival in Egypt metaphorically and physically was exactly with the complexity anyone will imagine.

Aside from the outer appearance of my life achievements, I was still longing for the arrival to a place that belonged to me and I could call home. My destination was Egypt Nile—the manifestation I put on my dream board every year on New Year's Day, the reincarnation of me in the best possible way, the little girl I had dreamed of visualizing all my life.

You see my journey was full of turbulence and opposition. So many times, I thought I would never arrive to my desired destination, or that I would even die during travel. To everyone's dismay (even mine) I arrived in better condition than how I departed from which I gained reverence for a greater power, a sense of purpose and never-ending exploration of a healthy life and destiny.

In the early days, defeat, abuse, guilt, and shame were my vehicles of choice navigating through life. An unconscious longing for self-defeat took me exactly where you would imagine—to a life without purpose, repeat heartache, and disappointment.

With love and understanding, I offer myself in the most vulnerable and transparent view to allow any woman, desiring inner freedom and the release of pain and restlessness, a peek into striving for wellness and eternal health. Believing that it is possible is the first course of action.

Loss and delay were divinely orchestrated in my life to create an outcome I never imagined I would ever have had. The understanding of life's failures and hurt can be just the correct vehicles to take you to a life that you deserve, but only with the willingness to work on self and understand the obstacles we all are faced with at one time or another.

As I relive the complicated life lessons and the intense gain of self-love, I only can share my incredible realization of a process that took me to a place I could not have dreamed of ever being: whole, healthy, and vigilant about me.

Finally, I got it! Release from self-defeating encounters, self-limiting thoughts and a plan to turn my failures into successes.

It is true that there is no value you can place on time; it's our most valuable commodity we all possess, but it's also true that, when happiness and consciousness is obtained, no amount of time is **ever** lost.

As I look in the mirror today, I rejoice, and I am thankful for every hardship and experience that brought me here. How many times I cried out asking why! Why must I suffer? why am I experiencing repeated lessons? Those vehicles of loss and dismay were my vehicle to arrive exactly where I needed to be at precisely the time I needed to be there.

I can remember during my nursing school education, studying American theorist <u>Abraham Maslow</u> that created **Maslow's hierarchy of needs**, a behavioral theory that we were required to study and recall associated with human behavior. We were tested on our remembrance of the steps listed in the theory and the chronological order of each level.

Reflecting back, I remember the theorist depiction always being illustrated in the form of a pyramid yet I had no real understanding of this behavioral theory in relation to my life. It was not until years later that I realized a pyramid had been in my subconscious forever, and I began to revisit the categories of the classification system of motivation.

- Physiological Needs. Food, water, clothing, sleep, and shelter are the bare necessities for anyone's survival.
- Safety and Security. Once a person's basic needs are satisfied, the want for order and predictability sets in.
- Love and belonging.
- Esteem.
- Self-Actualization.

One of the first thoughts that comes to mind when thinking of a pyramid is the country of Egypt and the pyramids of Giza. I didn't know how incredibly symbolic the pyramid was in theory nor how much significance it would hold in my life.

The notion of moving upward from the lowest level of the pyramid and ascending to the top reaching your desired place in life is a comparison that I like to adopt and use. The concept is simple; however, the act can be a challenge to climb upwards to reach the top of our existence—just as mountaineers take the literal physical adventure to climb actual mountains in nature. Any mountaineer that plans to climb a mountain considers what equipment is needed to make it successful. The mountaineer uses specifically constructed climbing boots, rope, and, most importantly, rescue gear.

During our climb to places desired in life, we also need to arm ourselves with some important equipment to arrive at the desired level. Optimizing our emotional wellness and gathering tools that expand our understanding is a major component and need. Unexpected challenges will occur. However, the use of The Trinity Strategy daily will ensure success.

Time at each level is self-determined and decided by the individual making the journey. For some it can be an expeditious trip and for others it can take a lot longer to ascend to the desired level. For myself, it was a long, yet worthwhile, hike. My climb was not smooth nor easy, but, thankfully, I accepted the invitation and made the ascending rise. I am a firm believer that life obstacles do not prevent success; they give us the motivation to achieve success.

Understanding my self-worth and determining exactly what this entailed took hard work, time, patience, and, most of all, the will to persevere. I felt I had lost so much time learning the lessons and developing the tools that ultimately gave birth to the place I stand in now, but, in all actuality, it was just the path and vehicle I used to ascend my pyramid. During my research, I discovered a condensed daily formula that makes ascending your life pyramid untroubled and most importantly achievable.

The word bankruptcy most often is associated with monetary status; however, I know what it means to be emotionally bankrupt with no more to give and a sense of lack to extend to others that are selfishly demanding the use of your inner strength. Multiple dysfunctional relationships intensified my emotional lack. I was giving from an empty account— an account that had not been funded, replenished, or managed properly to allow a healthy deposit into anyone else because I had mismanaged my own emotional funding. I had not invested the time into my core self that I deserved. Consequently, I had no emotional bank or emotional understanding. To fund yourself requires the same principle as starting a monetary bank account: a deposit. It is saving a required amount or depositing small percentages from your earnings to start an account. It is the same concept just with different deposit material. Your ability to build emotional wealth is determined by what you do daily to enhance your inner self. Whether you are employed or own your own company for means of income, your action generates revenue. Performing daily action just as you perform action to earn money generates emotional wealth. Emotional wealth is something that grants a true ability to meet every need in your life. Obtaining emotional substance gives birth to the possibilities of obtaining whatever desires you have; rather, it is a better lifestyle, a life partner, success, or happiness. The possibilities are endless. The investment in ourselves is the most important investment we can make. Without self-preservation. we cannot give to anyone. It is simply impossible.

My desire to save a person and become his perfect woman led me to give despite not having emotional clarity and wellness for myself. These irresponsible actions took me from deficit to deficit.

I had such a strong willingness to be accepted by the men in my life it overshadowed my inner desires to truly evaluate what I needed and wanted. I was being fueled by his passions and his needs. My needs were unimportant and insignificant.

This phenomenon is not foreign or unheard of. Rather, it is far too common in the lives of women seeking love and acceptance. That acceptance can be from a mate, a job, or lifestyle that we so desperately desire to make us feel validated. Subconsciously, we are all seeking happiness, peace, and solace. There is nothing wrong with wanting validation; however, attempting to get it with outside accomplishments without first investing in ourselves is problematic. What seems to be unfamiliar to most women is how we can stop this self-limiting attitude and place importance on self without feeling a sense of unfulfillment.

During my young adulthood, I was much too concerned about the outlook someone else possessed of me and very rarely considered myself important in relationships with peers. My need for acceptance trumped my need to genuinely love myself.

Where did this flaw come from? My judging myself from someone else's vision? Perhaps it was the absent inconsistent father relationship during childhood or environment perhaps it was simply not being taught traditional self-value. Over the years, I have investigated the possibilities of why I was so prone to the multiple pitfalls I landed in and whatever the was at fault. It was clear early on I would not have a productive, happy life if it did not include prioritizing myself.

I find so many similarities of myself in the young women I now work with—the normalcy of engaging in self-defeating behavior while attempting to create a sense of value is such a common practice in so many women.

I can remember meeting a beautiful, young lady who was brought into the Emergency Department of the hospital I was then working at. She was young, beautiful and oozing with potential. She was brought in for emergency care after experiencing a physical assault by her then boyfriend. She was so ashamed at what had transpired she was slumped down in the gurney avoiding much if any eye contact with anyone. I was assigned as her nurse and began to converse with her about what was currently happening in her life.

The day she was brought into the hospital she was dressed in loose athletic gear and a knit hat that was pulled down low, almost covering her eyes. I gave her a gown and asked her to change into it while I stepped out. When I returned, she had donned the gown and was sitting in the gurney looking downward. I noticed the knit hat remained on her head and I thought, "Well, maybe her hair is messy and she doesn't want to take it off." However, since the main complaint was that she had been hit repeatedly in the head by her boyfriend, we needed the hat to be removed for an examination. I said to her, "Can you take your hat off so we can see what's going on with your head?" She was reluctant to do so. I assured her, "I'm not here to judge you and don't care about your hair being a mess." She said, "No, that's not why I don't want to take it off." I said, "What is it then? We need to make certain that everything is okay and even get a CT scan of your head for possible internal bleeding." She reluctantly pulled the hat off while looking at me with tears in her eyes. When she removed the hat, it revealed the area she had been hiding: a tattoo above her eye of a man's name. The same man that had placed her in this condition. "I'm so mad at myself for getting this tattoo. I knew I shouldn't have gotten it, but he begged me to get it and said it would prove I belonged to him forever."

In that moment, I felt a sadness and saw a reflection of myself within her. We began to talk, and she expressed feelings of why she continued to stay in this type of relationship. She said, "He's the only one I ever felt like loved me. We used to spend so much time together. He never wanted to be apart from me, but now it's totally different. He gets mad at me when I want to go someplace with him and says I'm too clingy."

I shared my many struggles with self-worth and my active journey to define my authentic self and cultivate my self-awareness. This young lady was smart, sweet, and deserved so much more. However, her understanding of her worth was nonexistent. After our meeting in the hospital, I began to work with her, encouraging her to explore her feelings and to gain an identity different than what her boyfriend had labeled her as. As time went on and we grew to know each other better, she revealed that not only had she fallen victim to his physical abuse, but he had been prostituting her out for sex.

Years have passed since our initial meeting and this beautiful girl spent years of working on herself. She went through ups and downs, but, today, she is pursuing a college degree and gainfully employed. She found her true self. She is happy and making strides to be the woman she wants to become.

Who we are is the most important understanding we can ever gain. It is true that we must learn skills to effectively navigate through life, but it is all totally irrelevant if we achieve skills without genuine knowledge of our inner selves. It is like walking through a maze with instructions and no rationale for why we are doing it and, moreover, where the road is leading you.

You can gain a variety of exterior achievements without feeling fulfilled. Obtaining material items and achieving status quo does not give happiness or peace. Your ability to understand your emotions and awareness of self gives you the ability to obtain whatever it is you desire from an informed standpoint. It removes the probability of operating from an illusion. When we know ourselves, we do not need to worry about becoming involved in subject matter that we will later regret or spend time repairing. The foundation is laid, and the manual for life challenges is precise and authentic.

Life events occur from the time of birth until the departure of life. There is no magic performance that prevent situations from taking place; however, self-awareness grants us everything needed to meet the challenge and heal the pain that may come from these events.

It is preposterous to ask a visitor for directions to some place in a city he has never been and expect a correct outcome. It is the same concept when we look outside of ourselves for correct directions to the place we desire to go.

Losing a child is one of the most devastating things a woman could endure. Something ripped from your being that is part of you and the natural innocence you possess. In 1999, I lost my love, my Cookie. She arrived so pure and beautiful, yet lifeless, without breath in her body. How am I going to make it through this? Is all I ever thought. How will I escape the internal hurt that plagued my entire existence?

The journey began. My awakening for healing, peace, and solitude, the circumstances under which she was born, were less than ideal and full of negativity and distress. The relationship I was involved in was toxic, abusive, and dysfunctional. I had endured years of physical and emotional abuse in the relationship prior to her conception. I had chosen a man that was not present emotionally and my intense need for acceptance worsened the negative treatment I continually desired.

My thoughts were "She's my only hope," "How can I possibly exist without her," but her coming to me for that ever-so-brief moment gave me the first tool to exist with purpose and a desire for a healthier existence. It is important that we understand that, no matter how harsh the event is, we have the power of standing in gratitude for what we do have. During my darkest hour with grief and sorrow overwhelming me, I experienced a tiny feeling of gratitude. I was thankful that I could hold her, thankful that I could see her. Even though I was engulfed with intense sadness, gratitude somehow was there in the moment.

When faced with a traumatic, tragic event, no one ever dreams at the time it occurs that such a tragic experience will lead to any form of positivity. Our brains instinctively focus on the hurt and trauma the event has caused.

When the normal process of grief begins, we can go through a series of adverse emotions, none of which initially provides a sense of consolation or solace. After the trauma the emotions of denial, anger, and depression consumed me. My significant loss halted my previous acceptance of abuse—physically, mentally, and emotionally. It became unacceptable. Setting my eyes upon my child with gratitude and sorrow allowed me to identify a feeling of worth within myself. Gratitude took root when I gave life to her.

Until that turbulent moment, I had no self-worth. However, the jolt of losing, gaining, and losing simultaneously unblocked a door within my soul. I finally longed to include myself as a relevant part of the life I was living.

My quest to find the pureness I had witnessed so briefly when she came into the world was somewhere in my being. I had to set out to find any resemblance of what I felt when I held her those few hours after delivery. "She came from me so it's got to be in here somewhere," I would say.

I can remember the day my water broke at just 23 weeks of pregnancy. I had engaged in a heated argument with my child's father that morning. I was forced to begin a premature delivery with the knowledge that it was a next to impossible chance she would live. After delivering this stillborn angel, I held her for hours. My feelings were indescribable—I felt a sense of guilt that maybe this argument made this horrible event happen. All sorts of thoughts swirled in my mind. Every negative thought I had from recent days replayed in my memory. Wow, what did I do? What happens now? I felt intense sadness, but somehow a sense of strength came during the time I was able to hold and see her. I was so conflicted. How am I this weak and saddened and yet for the first time feel strength simultaneously? What is going on? I was in a position in which I had no ability or tools to begin to understand.

An overwhelming despair came when my family and the hospital staff urged me to allow her to be taken out of the room. "It's time now." "You need to say goodbye." I could not begin to verbalize my feelings to any of them. I felt no one could understand my complicated, tangled feelings and thoughts. I was alone in this journey.

My search for peace started with years of visiting Ashrams, synagogues, churches, and even temples. This led me to develop a plan to transform my hardships into healing.

It took exactly what I had experienced to reach the height of my pyramid. My hardships had placed me in a position that I could only rise upward. I was already at my low. I had experienced years of abuse, I had been scarred mentally and physically, and I had lost the one thing I held dearest to my heart.

My life had been saturated with turmoil. The thought of normalcy or birthing another child scared me to the depths of my soul. No, I could never consider the risk of experiencing love that pure and have it snatched away again. I would just work on myself and attempt to recreate the essence of what she showed me I possessed. My plan worked, and I captured a little glimpse of the pureness within that I had identified when I held my baby girl... But my brief encounter with motherhood that I thought was over had just begun.

Years went by as a I journeyed to be happy and free from the lies and false concepts I grew up believing. I rediscovered the arts through painting. Painting allowed me to express my feeling on canvas. I set out to address the "uncool things" I had an interest in. I painted, meditated, and wrote year after year, all while exploring my inner self that I had neglected so long.

Something was happening. I was changing, not my outer appearance but the thing that really mattered —my inner self, that I had neglected for so long. The immature girl was blossoming into a woman of worth and substance.

Suddenly, the once negative outlook I had on life and my unaddressed inner core had been discovered and was before me waiting to be cultivated.

Countless visits to spiritual retreats, meditation, and praying assisted me in creating a simple guide to stay in the moment and be true to the most important person on the journey, MYSELF.

The delicate transition from girl to woman leads me to understand that as people we have a responsibility in life to others that may have traveled a similar road. Vulnerability and kindness to share the traumas endured and triumphed over allows me to turn every obstacle into a success. I traveled a very intense journey, and my arrival to gratitude and wellbeing is something I celebrate every day. Through my expression of gratitude, I stand in a position of strength yet vulnerability that I engage in sharing my experiences in hopes of encouraging transformation in the same way I achieved with a condensed plan of daily measures to assist our consciousness to emerge and remain present.

(Journal entry)

Just once I would like to be accepted for who I am and respected for what I stand for, even if you don't quite understand me. Don't take advantage of someone because of the situation. Respect the person enough to provide them with what you desire... All or nothing at all. Make decisions that are consistent with your outlook on life. Be true to yourself and others even if that means making life a little difficult for yourself. Rely on you, don't expect people to responsibility for your being...not cool!

Upon reflecting on the above caption I wrote many years ago, I realize something quite interesting. I was complaining of being taken advantaged of without taking responsibility for my own self-understanding. It is impossible for anyone to respect you if you do not know how to respect yourself. I was guilty of not taking aside any time to gain self-awareness.

Lack of self-awareness places you in a position of not fully respecting yourself—your value is unknown. You can only value something if you understand its capabilities and functions. For example: The value that is placed on an expensive luxury car is done based on a consumer knowing its functions and capabilities The consumer has been made aware of what the vehicle potentially offers while driving or riding in it. The manufacturer knows the complete specifications of the vehicle. This concept is similar with self-knowledge. You cannot express your value to someone if you are unaware of it. The respect for self comes with understanding your personal potential and recognizing it. If we neglect to do so, we place ourselves in a position to subconsciously allow disrespect.

Some would argue that urban culture and lack of resources can prevent a woman from gaining a greater self-understanding, I, however, do not agree. A woman's ability to recognize responsibility for her life happens during times of hardship. No matter who you are and what upbringing you were raised with, no one person is exempt from experiencing pain or adverse life events.

A hardship gives an opportunity to examine ourselves at the most vulnerable and pivotal times. I am not suggesting that there is joy in trauma or a negative life event. However, the opportunity for growth exists in each adverse experience. Life is comprised of contrasts. Both good and bad is relevant. The ability to use these unpleasant experiences to capture greater meaning in life provides peace and fulfillment.

Inner emotions always seem complex during the developing years. I do not know if this is because things inside give an illusion that they are harder to distinguish, or we simply do not receive direct instruction on combatting the possible pitfalls.

The inner self is what guides and directs our outward appearance path and life. It would seem that at some point our inner being would be greater cherished and greater emphasis would be placed on how better to cultivate it, but it isn't. The emphasis is placed on the outcome—appearance of life successes and obtaining material things in life.

Self-awareness can be defined in a number of ways: having an understanding of yourself, understanding your value or plain knowing who you are is just a few definitions. The fact is self-awareness is our key to making the right decision for our life's path and ultimately obtaining happiness throughout our endeavors.

Following the clues given to us on the inside is a lot more productive than chasing outside trends and media hype that have no relevance to us individually. Through media, girls are given so many impossible guidelines to follow for being called cool or beautiful. The outside influences provide an unattainable goal to follow (for example, a character on a TV show or a model that makes her living maintaining her external beauty.) We are very seldom told to develop our own identity or what seems natural to us. As a result, so many of us walk through life imitating someone else or following the path considered to be cool and desirable. This false sense of living kills our genuine identity and lessens our understanding for what is real.

I fell victim to this syndrome. I grew up in Detroit, Michigan. A place that got cold in the winter and even hotter in the summer. My neighborhood was heavily influenced by fast cars, violence, and fast money. I bought into the entire street culture. I was mesmerized by street life and had no idea why. I hadn't spent any time developing who I was or even understanding what was important to me. I searched on the outside for everything I thought I may need in life. As a result, I chose what I saw in my environment: a difficult path. I fell victim to domestic violence and an utter disrespect for all that was good. I overlooked what my inner being was saying to me and looked outside for everything, even the values of who I should be and who to become.

Since the days prior, I have developed self-awareness and understand of who I am, but it was only through performing self-love activities that I gained insight of who I truly am and what is truly important to me. If we don't investigate our inner being and persist on developing our purpose, it becomes easy to adopt someone else's vision for your own.

Developing self-worth and self-awareness starts by taking an inventory of what seems natural and fitting to you despite what the trends and social influences display. An understanding of what is important to you and what your goals entail gives a good predictor of what your purpose is and where your path will continue.

One day, I was at home in LA, and my girlfriend was helping me get dressed for an event I was attending with a guy I was dating at the time. I had bought a few outfits to choose from and could not decide which one I wanted to wear. So like so many other women I asked my girlfriend to help me with her opinion. I changed into those outfits about ten times back and forth trying to decide what looked better. I was so undecided and I constantly kept asking my friend, "Which one looks better?" After she gave me her opinion countless times, she finally said, "Which one do you like? What are you going to feel more comfortable in?"

These were valid questions to ask myself to help me to make a decision on a dress. The crazy thing was, when I thought about it, my entire focus was not on what I liked to see myself in, but rather my thought process was on what my date would wanted to see me in. What was going to be sexier and more appealing to him was my primary concern. Now, I understand that everyone wants to be attractive for their mate, but constant consideration of everyone else's opinion as priority to yours is cause for concern. Second guessing your own opinion is beyond what is needed to be considered attractive by someone else. Conforming to societal norms and trends without taking into consideration your own comfort and feeling about yourself is hazardous. It may seem harmless in terms of choosing a style of dress. However, it indicates a need for greater understanding of self would be beneficial to you. Repeatedly embracing someone else's standards instead of your own is a sign to take action and research your authentic self.

Journaling
Step 1 of Your Path to Egypt

I don't know
Only God knows where the story ends for me
but I know where the story begins,
It's up to us to choose,
whether we win or lose
and I choose to win

~Mary J. Blige, *"No More Drama"*

Journaling is key for sorting out feelings, identifying areas for improvement, and getting clarity on life events. Writing down likes, dislikes, and goals creates a greater sense of understanding for who you are and strive to become. Write down honest answers. This is for your eyes only. You can focus on things relevant to your current life goals and write what it is you would like to see yourself accomplishing like finishing your education, obtaining a better job, buying a home, or just simply being kinder to yourself.

When I first began to journal, I wrote about significant things that were happening to me, good or bad. Whatever opposition I was facing or what my feelings were about the situation. I placed them on paper, expelling all emotion within me onto the outside. The sheer fact of releasing thoughts of relevance onto paper allows the brain to process the events with more clarity. Reading a thought or issue from a particular time gives a sense of retrospect that cannot be obtained from swirling mental thoughts inside.

I found that writing during turbulent times gave me a feeling of release. That somehow, I had removed some of the constant thoughts surrounding the issue at hand. It helped me write to myself in third party, asking questions of myself: Why is this bothering you so much? What would you like to see come of this situation? To your dismay, you will be surprised at the answers that come about when you ask yourself questions on paper. The ability to release the problem onto another canvas besides your brain allows you to think about situations from a different perspective. There are no rules to how you journal. Being present with your true feelings are all you need. It does not require any special format, just a few minutes throughout your day to take inventory on what is happening inside.

I have included excerpts of my journal writings throughout this book. Many times my writings were with markers, pencil, or whatever was around that I felt like using. I wrote down events that had an importance at that particular time in my life.

Before I discovered the connection to the Trinity Strategy I use today, I was writing my thoughts of how I felt during my traumatic life moments. I wrote many times about the loss of my daughter and the complicated thoughts I experienced. While I did not have all the answers, it provided the needed outlet to express things I could not express to anyone else. It does not matter how complex or unsure you are of the thoughts you write. They are yours and only for your review.

Journaling also provides multiple ways of building your self-esteem as well as your desired place in life. The focus on attributes you are seeking can also be used. Using words that you feel will make you better in your journey is key. The goal of journaling your thoughts is the positive outcome of feeling a sense of relief that these thoughts are being transferred outside of you into another area.

The simple act of writing the thought or situation gives the mind a needed rest from the wandering of thoughts, giving a place and time for the thought to be expelled outside of your mind. It is important to check in with ourselves daily, once before starting the day and once upon completion. Any other time are bonus entries and will provide satisfaction.

Consciousness is something we are in search of whether we realize it or not. As human beings, we all possess a natural desire to evolve into a greater dimension of life. There is no societal economic class that makes this innate desire obsolete or hidden. Our individuality creates unique directions and desired places we desire to be. However, subconsciously, we all desire to feel better and be at peace. It is sometimes difficult to believe when you see a person engaging in self-destructive activities or lifestyle choices. These self-limiting practices are being done to achieve a sense of fulfillment.

We can take a meaningful word and begin to write about how the attribute fits in our existing life or how we visualize it to be.

- Gratitude
- Love
- Acceptance
- Perseverance
- Health
- Community
- Success
- Opportunity
- Peace
- Understanding
- Strength
- Kindness

Writing attributes that bring about positive feeling changes our energy and focus. Words are powerful in a spoken context as well as when we write them. You can write words of your choice and what makes these attributes important to you. Ask the questions that focus on how you can increase this quality in your life. Questions like: What steps can I take to experience these attributes in my life? How can I perform an unprovoked act of kindness? Perhaps offering a compliment to someone, aiding someone in need.

Being of service to others can ignite a positive portal within of not only giving kindness but also receiving positivity from others around you.

Here are some journal examples that will be helpful in identifying what traits you already own and identify ones you are interested in developing.

I'm proud that I possess...

1. _____

2. _____

3. _____

4. _____

I admire these qualities in others and look forward to them being a part of who I am:

1. _____

2. _____

3. _____

The single most important quality within me is:

_____

At the end of this book, there is a 30-day plan for daily check-in morning & evening.

Developing a regular journaling schedule allows you the ability to both expel and review answers to various life questions. Writing your honest thoughts on various situations and experiences will provide insight on what is innately important to you and what areas you need to focus on further. In any event, whether the expressions you write are all joyous and happy does not matter because the reason you are exploring your inner being is for the love of self, and the outcome will prove to be a positive one.

The journaling schedule is completely your choice. The more you can put your thoughts onto paper the better. You may choose to extensively journal once per week. However, it is imperative that you check in with yourself daily. I recommend writing briefly before the day begins and before bed, after it is complete. This provides the opportunity to check in and keep a physical record of what is going on day to day. It also tracks your progress for achieving the goal you are in pursuit of. I make it a point of keeping my journals from previous years for the purpose of reflection. I can remember sitting down during the beginning of the New Year 2017 and reading some of my journal entries written over 5 years prior. I was so shocked, thankful, and amazed that I had achieved almost everything on my wish list. I recommend creating a wish list every five years.

At the time, I had wrote countless goals and the main ones were for buying property, increasing my income, and traveling to Africa. On the day I reflected, I had obtained those goals and more. To read your prior writing and creations is like visiting a person and time you know very well. You will find that as time passes and you delve inwards, you will evolve into a new you.

The goal is to explore your feelings as often as possible. The beautiful thing about journaling is that it is continuous. You do not have to feel pressured to complete any journal entry because you always have the ability to pick back up where you left off.

In modern times, people will often type and text messages. However, effective journaling requires us to engage, using our hands with a pen or pencil, allowing the physical movement to meet our brain activity. This movement allows your brain to retain the connection with your heart.

2015 painting I created entitled *Fertile Moments*

What I See in the Mirror
Step 2 of Your Path to Egypt

If you change the way you look at things, you look at change.
~Dr. Wayne Dyer

There are multiple ways to increase self-awareness and maintain an understanding of valuing self. One of our favorite practices we do during workshops at FIG is called *What I See in the Mirror*. It is a very simple technique, yet extremely effective, for enhancing what we already know about ourselves.

Activity:

- Take a face-size mirror and place it to your face. Without any distractions, begin to gaze into the reflection of your face.
- Note any feelings that may come up while performing this act. You may find that you instinctively start to examine a part of your face

with a criticizing thought. For example, *Wow, my skin is oily* or *where did this pimple come from?* Stay focused, and remind yourself that you are looking deeper than the surface.

The object of the activity is not to assess your exterior beauty or flaws but rather to tell yourself about the positive characteristics that lie within.

Performing this activity enhances the positive attributes that we all possess. You may start with telling yourself the first positive descriptive word that comes to mind and proceed from there. During this activity, you should give yourself a minimum of three positive words to find about yourself. It is important that, before beginning this exercise, the ground rule should be established that no negative words are allowed.

I can recall working with a young lady at a workshop. During this activity, she had such a difficult time with finding descriptive words that did not pertain to her external appearance or accomplishments.

The first words that came to mind were about her hair, lips, and eyebrows, not the core description that really defined her as a woman. We are so programmed to focus on our outer appearance, the features a person sees when they look at you, that our true inner self goes unacknowledged and unexamined. It is easy to start to believe that our physical self is what is most important.

We all understand that the first thing a person sees is your physical appearance. Just because it is the initial sight does not make it more significant. Who we are is greater defined by what we possess within ourselves. If steps are not taken to have a full understanding of our genuine selves, our identity can be misplaced, and our physicality can take precedence.

Media outlets have lent so many varying ideas of what is pleasing, acceptable, and attractive. Women have been given unrealistic guides and made up story lines for life that are designed to create the standard of beauty, success, and worth, all without the focus of inner beauty, emotional health, and wellness.

Taking an interest in pursuing our inner qualities and self-beauty leads to life accomplishments, success, and, most importantly, happiness.

Kenya Lee

AFFIRM
Second Part of Step 2 of Your Path to Egypt

Often, we act as our own worst critic with giving ourselves self-limiting thoughts and the pressure of being and doing everything perfectly. A conscious way to maintain an equilibrium is to take a deliberate positive inventory of ourselves and recite these characteristics to ourselves.

Reciting simple positive affirmations can ignite the lost fire of who we know our true self to be or provide us to a pathway of obtaining what we desire. Positive words are powerful tools that we often take for granted and discount the power they hold. Speaking affirmations can change your mood and also manifest any change you may desire in your life. Simply stating what you know to be true or what you desire to change creates a shift in consciousness that penetrates our being and reminds us of our higher self. After all, if we can act as a self-critic, we should also be able to self-motivate!

During my initial years of working with a therapist, I discovered how extremely challenging, yet life changing, it became when I stated simple positive things to myself. Each time my therapist would give me affirmations to repeat, like "I am worthy of love," or "I am willing to accept love," an uncontrollable feeling of fear and emotion would come over me when I attempted to say the affirmations with conviction. The first couple of times, I cried intensely.

Repetition of these affirmations facilitated the feeling of fear to transform to comfort; however, I could not help but ask myself the question: do I deep down really think so little of myself? The evidence of my life decisions pointed in that direction, but, from a conscious thought and without intense pondering, I could not see the reasons behind it all. What was happening to me on a deeper level that was not visible? How did the act of verbally speaking a positive statement bring about so much emotion?

I had unknowingly bought into the criticisms and put downs that had been handed to me over time. A negative hold had taken root on my mental outlook of myself and the mere speaking against it stirred something up deep within.

Negative baggage that often attaches itself to us during childhood and adolescence remain with us as truth until we take an active role in redirecting it into the appropriate places. Feelings of being unworthy and not good enough unfortunately plague women during various times of growth as we attempt to discover a place of acceptance in society.

Taking an active role to create compassion and forgiveness for ourselves by way of active self-love activities is the best way to reprogram our emotions and achieve inner acceptance. Daily positive affirmations remind us of how incredibly powerful we are as women. You can create your own specific affirmations to give your inner self information about the person you are. This will provide positive energy that will help guide you to your desired destination.

AFFIRMATIONS

- *I am enough.*
- *I am fearless.*
- *I am deserving of love in its purest form.*
- *I am confident.*
- *I am getting better every day.*
- *I am filled with gratitude.*
- *I have what I need inside of me.*

- *I am living in abundance.*
- *I am motivated.*
- *I have a positive impact on the people I come in contact with.*
- *I rise above thoughts that try to make me angry and afraid.*
- *I am intelligent.*
- *I am focused.*
- *I am healing and getting stronger every day.*
- *My past doesn't define me.*
- *Peace is within me.*
- *I am strong.*
- *I am resilient.*
- *Perfection is not realistic but my best is good enough.*
- *Happiness is a choice and I choose to be happy.*

During busy life, we tend to forget about the qualities we possess within us. Choosing a daily affirmation before beginning our day helps set the mood of how we will complete our day. Placing a truthful positive thought at the forefront of our minds allows us to tackle whatever situations we face with the knowing we have what is needed to succeed.

Affirmations can be written specifically for what you need to focus on. They do not have to be general; they can be constructed for your own personal situation. Examples:

I have what I need within to obtain the promotion I want at work.

I am open to love, and I will recognize it when I see it.

I finish what matters and let go of what doesn't.

I focus my mind and I feed my spirit; I am becoming healthier.

What would you like to affirm to yourself when starting your day:

1. _____

2. _____

3. _____

4. _____

5. _____

6. _____

7. _____

8. _____

9. _____

10. _____

Domestic Violence

Your willingness to look at your darkness is what empowers you to change.

~Iyanla Vanzant

Domestic violence is a term that recently has been changed to intimate partner violence. No matter how it is termed, it is a subject that I know a great deal about. For several years, I took part in toxic relationships that, time after time, resulted in violence. During the times I endured such violence, I often speculated why I gravitated to an abuser as the love of my life. When the truth of the matter was I was like a magnet for anyone looking to control someone. An abuser is always looking for someone with little or no self-esteem. Little did I know I was not doing such a great job hiding the fact that I was a girl more concerned with what a man thought about me rather than how I felt about myself. I always aimed to keep a strong exterior; however, the truth always prevails, and, unfortunately, my low self-awareness was identified by men that aimed to control me. It was not until I began to take steps to gain worth and purpose that I was able to remove the label seen so readily by potential abusers.

> ### (Journal entry)
>
> *"I lost my only love, myself. I feel I am shackled by dead weight. I have compromised myself so much in this relationship that I somehow will never reap what I've sown into this crazy cycle and maybe that's because it was never supposed to be. I allowed youth to guide me in a circle of madness and confusion but once I elevated my understanding it would seem I would have walked away but it didn't happen. My happiness has not been top priority... Why? I was willing to stand by him through uncertainties... Why, couldn't I offer the same to me?*

Reflecting on a past journal entry, I see that I was a girl with a simple understanding that I was in a relationship that was bad for me; however, I was so out of touch with who I was and what my worth consisted of I felt I could not walk away from the bad decisions I had allowed to be part of my existence. I felt trapped to continue to endure the negativity. Despite having the physical ability to walk away, my mental and emotional stagnation prevented me from seeing any alternatives for a better life. My unhealthy mindset did not even grant me the desire to want more only to keep me battling with self-destruction.

Women understanding that our worth is no less significant than a man's desire. Practicing self-awareness in everyday life is most important when combatting domestic violence. Obtaining self-esteem allows us to gain care and respect for ourselves ultimately giving priority to self over anyone or anything.

Violence between intimate partners can rear its ugly head in a variety of ways. It does not always have to be physical. There are several areas abusers take advantage. Domestic abuse is categorized as physical, sexual, emotional, economic, or psychological.

The one characteristic that all categories of abuse have in common is that control is at the base of all intent. Recognizing the warning signs for domestic violence can help identify a potential abuser before any abuse takes place and gives women the tools to escape the situation.

Warning Signs

The subtle behaviors that I should have recognized as warning signs from my abusers were wrongly perceived as intense caring. I quite naively dismissed questions like: "Where are you going?", "How long are you going to be?" from someone that cared intensely for me. When the reality was this behavior for wanting to know my every move was a sign that he wanted to maintain control of me and limit my ability to explore life outside his standard.

(Journal entry)

As a woman that didn't grow up with my father or strong male influences, I accepted any attention that was shown by a male towards me in whatever capacity I could obtain it. My idea of a father is to love, guide and gently correct his children. A father helps his daughter to understand the importance of life and also sets the standard of how a man should treat her.

> *Unfortunately, I had no personal standard to reference so I looked for character traits that possibly resembled the behavior of a father.*

Behavior like demanding that I changed clothes prior to leaving the house or removing makeup because he felt it was inappropriate was initially received as just a jealous guy that cared a lot for his girlfriend. It was not until the newness wore off and the requests became frequent demands that the trouble began.

My comments of opposition and inability to understand why I had to change myself so often was met by explosive anger. Slowly these angry discussions about my appearance escalated to physical episodes of slapping and hitting to make me change whatever he had a problem with.

There are several warning behaviors that suggest a person has the capability to be an abuser besides control. The most common are:

- Humiliate or put you down
- Criticize you or your accomplishments
- Ignore your opinions
- Blame you for their abusive behavior

- View you as property or a sex object
- Destroy your belongings
- Keep you from seeing your friends & family
- Threaten to harm himself or you if you leave

Educating ourselves about these warning signs of abuse can allow us to recognize what may come later. Let's not take on the position that we can change the person or minimalize the unacceptable behavior because we like the person. Understand we cannot change anyone; we have control over only ourselves.

(Journal entry)

I give you this gift to provide a map—atlas—so you will never get lost again. Keep to the plan. Do not allow circumstances you have no control over to dictate your next move or if you move. Allow trust to emerge from the unknown and go with nature's trail, knowing this is the correct one for you; understanding you will get exactly what you want.

My life at one time was composed of circular movements. I operated by repeating exact lessons over and over again. People on the outside could see what the disturbance was and so could I, at times; however, I chose to hold on to the false belief that I could make it better. The truth of it all was I had no more control to make the toxic relationship better than I had over the toxins that pollute the air in the world.

> ### (Journal entry)
>
> *I'm so mad at myself for indulging in a relationship with him. I knew better! I'm so close to giving up every dream and aspiration I've ever had. No one knows how I feel—to be lost and have special dreams you were promised would come forward and have it never happen, don't want to cry and give up but what choice do I have besides staying and not knowing my left from right?*

I did have control of myself. So why is it so difficult to break away from the hurt? I pondered this question many times without getting a clear, concise understanding until the magic of Faith happened. I became pregnant with a daughter, and, despite all of my many decisions to have abortions that came before, I decided to complete this pregnancy and finally became a mother. I had somehow thought that the birth of a child would possibly create a life change that would offer positivity. The birth of my daughter did exactly what I had hoped, but not before a difficult reality happened first. My daughter was stillborn, without any breath in her tiny body, and although she would not remain with me for a lifetime, her short visit proved to be exactly what I needed and desired: a way out of the unhealthy, toxicity that plagued my entire existence.

My escape did not happen overnight nor was it an easy road to endure, but, by God, it happened! An awakening and surging of energy penetrated my entire being. The answers that I had been searching for in my environment and relationship mysteriously revealed that they were inside me the entire time. The work was going to be beckoning them out so that I could take full advantage of what they offered: my life's purpose. A series of events had to happen before I was able to come into this realization. I first had to grieve this substantial loss of my child and also grieve the loss of living life from the outside in.

I went through a series of stages before arriving at acceptance. During this time, I underwent the actual stages of death and dying. Death of the barriers that kept me from reaching into a new life.

I first experienced denial that my daughter's death was not a pivotal moment asking me to change something; maybe, just maybe, this was something that just happened! The more I denied the obvious fact that it was time for a life change, the angrier I became.

I progressively slipped into the stage of intense anger. I was angry that my life seemed to be in shambles, angry that my plans for a toxic family lifestyle had failed, but, most of all, angry that I had no control for reliving the events that had led up to that very moment. How had I arrived here? As I continued to harp heavily on not having control over her birth and death combined, bargaining quickly became the next stage I had to contend with. I asked God time and time again to please just change what had happened, and I promised to do everything perfectly. When days turned into weeks and weeks turned into months, I gave up the seemingly never-ending plea and dived into a state of depression.

I could not rise up on a daily basis, I lost all interest in life, suddenly the intense care I had for the man in my life vanished. I cared about nothing or no one but her memory and thoughts of her departing my arms. Whenever I found the strength to get up, the only place I could go was to her grave, lying there in the grass for days on end with no control over my Faith's passing. The depression was real and the tumultuous hurt from the depression opened a tiny door that asked, "What happens now?" The acceptance had appeared, and, suddenly, it was time to act on the gift that was being offered to me.

I cannot take a backseat to life anymore. This has happened for a reason. What am I doing here? Who will I become? What is this all about? If I continue living without purpose or understanding, her visit will have been in vain. That cannot be. I cannot endure the thought of this tragic event happening for no reason; however, the routine of negative living seemed to be an ingrained pattern that fought with intensity whenever I attempted to do something productive. I made the decision to pursue the inner awareness and set out to make progress.

Pursuing the goal of becoming a nurse had appealed to me since the days of childhood when I wanted to dress as a nurse on Halloween year after year. Chaos and turbulence always interrupted and lessened my passion to complete my academic journey. My focus on everything other than me had always taken priority.

Suddenly, the lights came on, and the path became dimly lit. I gathered every droplet of strength I had within and put it into pursuing my education. This new passion proved to be inviting and safe as I immersed myself and channeled the hurt into knowledge.

While I learned more academically, something happened internally. I started learning more about myself. I really did not need to be controlled and told what to do by a man; I was beyond capable of leading a successful, positive life. Upon completion of each academic challenge, a revelation would emerge about why I had adopted my former way of thinking and why I no longer desired it.

The answers to some of my questions slowly rose from within when I took the time to invest the interest that I saw so important to offer to a man. Wow! what a pivotal moment! I think I can operate without the self-inflicted hurt.

It was not long after receiving the understanding that my inner being guided my path in life and determined my results in life that I decided to nurture the one thing that could guarantee me wellness and success: ME. I made plans to take a job across country and practice nursing while I also practiced self-love for the first time.

Embarking upon an adventure that included putting all my trust into the person I had ignored for a lifetime proved to be both a challenge and a success. The work was not over. It was just beginning. Getting acquainted with who I really was and not following the image I had selected to follow was the most significant change. Daily writing and reflecting is part of the process. Providing the one thing I desired from others: love. Love of self is the cure all for everything that ails us as women.

(Journal entry)

I'm trying to work on me, satisfying the child within me. I want to feel good when I look in the mirror. Whenever I pray to God I neglect asking for what I want because I feel like I'm begging to someone tormenting me on purpose not providing happiness. I know I've done wrong and a lot of wrong has been done but how long will this go on until I'm tired and give up all expectations?

Gratitude for harsh realities and life's challenges awakens a part of me that desires to help every girl with the view that people and the external environment as the answer to life's questions as I once did.

I set out to create a curriculum and platform for sharing my struggles and realizations with girls in hopes they may be able to embrace self-awareness, ultimately bypassing self-neglect. I created a curriculum and an organization in Faith's name (Faith in Girls, Inc.), since she had been the wakeup call that led me to love myself. (To learn more, visit www.faithingirls.org)

One day, while attending a lecture on the topic of public health issues, I made the acquaintance of a lady with a very different story but the same passion for educating girls about life choices. This woman spoke with poise and concern about issues that led her to become a public educator. She was a woman that had overcome many difficulties in her life, like foster care and molestation. However ,the one issue that she was most passionate about was the issue she was living with day after day: HIV. She was HIV positive and a survivor of sixteen years. Even though Lori had major health concerns and posed the risk of opportunistic infections at times, she still made the commitment to go various places within different communities to educate youth on HIV myths and truths. Her dedication and willingness to share herself prompted me to ask her to join me in my crusade to reach young women to provide education on the importance of self.

The introduction of HIV in my life has been up close and personal. My uncle was diagnosed with HIV fourteen years ago, and I was present and active during the initial days of his seeking treatment, I learned the myths and truths about the disease but also witnessed the stigmas that accompanied a person that was HIV positive. I was extremely grateful to meet someone like Lori with the desire to educate young women on such an important topic that affected each and every one of us. We joined forces and have been providing educational workshops to girls and young women in the Los Angeles, California, area ever since. I look around and am so thankful for the wonderful invitation I have been given to shed light within the universe. My little contribution in the world is fulfilling my heart with the understanding of why life's events unfolded the way they did. It was not because I was a bad person or I had committed some evil deed. It was an avenue to get my attention and direct my focus onto something that had purpose and worth: ME.

Cool Factor

After embracing my authentic self, the interests that my environment deemed were not cool and that I had abandoned as a girl decided to surprisingly resurface. The artist in me wanted to express something that could not otherwise be communicated.

As a child, I was fond of art and classical music. By the age of eight, I wanted to paint by numbers and sculpt clay figures on my makeshift pottery wheel. Each time a commercial would come on advertising a musical play like *Evita* or *Phantom of the Opera*, I would scream with excitement and requested to attend. My requests were not taken too seriously, and, soon, the ideas of what others considered cool took precedence and my genuine importance was lost. The exact same thing had happened in my adult life when my feelings of self were disregarded and replaced by my environmental societal norms. What a tragedy having lost so many years of artistic expression simply because I did not know how to love myself in the genuine form, but, wow, what an exciting milestone discovering it almost for the first time!

I had recently moved to LA and wanted to embrace something new and different, so I decided to enroll in a class of some sort. I saw a listing for an art class listed in an area college directory called "Healing Arts." I thought I definitely need to heal and I always loved to paint. I thought, "I think I'll try it," and I discovered my lost, little girl I had left behind many years ago. The stories that my paintings told and the messages that they conveyed were far beyond my ability to communicate into words.

The instructor Patricia Thompson was an artist that lived her entire life introducing the miraculous world of art to others. Her intuition and ability to teach students how to interpret what they were expressing through paint was phenomenal. Her guidance taught me the ability to understand that silent communication through color, texture, and shape. What did I feel when viewing the finished product? What symbols or characters had emerged into the color and texture of the painting?

Here it was again, the inner being proving to be in control and having the ability to explain it all. Whenever I recognized the answers to the tough questions with this, my ability from within my understanding was reinforced. What a magnificent gift we all possess, creating visual art on a blank canvas. It expels what the spoken word cannot begin to explain—a look at the hidden pieces.

I began to want to paint outside of the classes I took formally. I headed to the art supply store and purchased a few canvas and ten bottles of acrylic paints and some brushes. The peace of mind I gained while painting was phenomenal! I would put on my music and create for hours. It felt like I was another person painting abstractly. I placed lines and color wherever I felt they should go. There was no rhyme or reason for how I began to create my art, only the feelings that fueled me in the moment. Painting left to right, up, down with no preset intent for what the painting had to be. My creations were messy, tangled, full of color and expression. My inner unconsciousness spilled onto canvas and stared back at me for my review. There was so much mystery and depth to what I created. Everything I possessed inside was being made clear each time I created a piece. The various symbols intrigued me. I wanted to see more so I painted continuously during my times of self-discovery.

As a child, I was never any good at drawing. I would color and doodle with crayon as most children do. Here I stood as an adult in the same way, but uniquely different, because my hands and mind were connecting to draw unconscious clues that spoke volumes of information about myself.

One day, while listening to music at my apartment, I set out to begin another abstract painting. I chose four colors for my newest creation. I took the colors red, gold, brown, and white out and began my process of painting. I began to move and place color wherever I felt it should be on my canvas. Hours passed since I had begun. I lost track of time during my creative flow. To my dismay, I had created quite an unusual painting that was full of objects and tones I could not clarify initially. I placed my project on hold like I so often did, waiting for the next block of time I could spare to paint.

A week or more past by before I was able to get back to my painting. I began a new session; my intent was to finish what I had started. My session began, and I was completely consumed in my process. My soft motivation song played as I sat and painted as I never had before.

As I began to get close to finishing the entire canvas, I visualized someone standing in grand form and clothed in royal attire. I was simultaneously excited and intrigued. I could not believe what I was seeing and that I had created this. Oh, my God! Who is that? It appears to be a lady, possibly a queen. I continued to paint and finish the canvas with color.

I stared at this painting in amazement. I had painted many times before but never had I expelled a figure any piece I had painted.

This lady had been birthed from my unconsciousness. She was a true representation of me and the strength I really possessed. My class in healing arts taught me how to examine and interpret my creations for the purpose of gaining clarity within my true self. This piece gave the surprising

discovery that I was a queen.
The king may rule the kingdom, but it's the queen who moves the board.~D.M. Timney

2015. "The Queen" She emerged onto my canvas. She lived inside of me all along.

(Journal entry)

My creativity is full of awareness that asks for more than the love and loss I've endured in life. I never imagined my expectancy would evolve so drastically. Memory of a lesser self often creeps into my thoughts yet I keep the understanding that the past sharpens what becomes. Arrival to an unvisited place is within reach.

What wonderful beginnings will emerge from the thoughts sent out with purpose. I'm loving this remarkable hour of life.

My continuous desire to create enhances my understanding of myself and adds to the insight I so greatly respect when working with girls and women that are reaching for their purpose in life. Learning about oneself is a lifelong process. No matter what level of self-understanding you achieve, you will be amazed at the additional insight that is obtained when the deliberate seeking of self is maintained.

Multiple studies have shown art to be an effective therapy for the release of traumas suffered by people physically, emotionally, and mentally. I had heard many people speak positively about the effect art presented them while undergoing challenging life events; however, I personally found the truth of this fact out by chance. Once I committed to creating art regularly, I noticed an immense sense of release that took place from within my inner being. I did not quite know exactly where it had released from; however, the finished project would consistently provide me clues to the mystery happening within me. I often experience a feeling of lightness and relief.

I was never a person that was capable of figuratively drawing, so any completed project that revealed a particular object was astounding. I never set out to draw anything only to expel the unknown subject that lies within. Shapes, letters, and actual images appear in my work, and each time something is recognized, it provides insight towards a life issue that needs additional addressing.

This insightful activity allows both the artist and viewer to be connected in an incredible way. My creations express the state of consciousness I resided in when I created the piece ultimately proving that art unifies and communicates organically without actual words.

(Journal entry)

Creating life with the materials that rest in our hands can sometimes be dirt, and gravel or pain. The point is it is all used as a medium for expression. So often the path we walk is filled with remnants from yesterday's events. Fire of spirit burns through the unwanted, leaving only blue skies and gray mountains. Stillness allows us to hear what we may have otherwise ignored.

Deciding to show up for life can seem like the hardest thing to do. I've accomplished so much yet it feels so little. I want to be rescued from the parables of defeat that surround my mind. I'm pushing myself to grab the positive that's right here in my presence yet the dread of possible defeat and failure seem imminent. The thoughts are completely false and an illusion. So, how do I proceed with the promise of success? Consistency in meditation is the only way that I will maintain an awake state without periods of drowsiness and desire of going back to the sleep of stagnation.

I understood what it meant to be still and quiet yet I did not have the precise understanding of the term meditation and what exactly it entailed.

During my upbringing in Detroit, religion was presented to me from a Christian perspective. The state of being still and quiet was associated with having the ability to hear from God. This was something I had often heard. However it wasn't described to me as a deliberate practice that required active participation. I had always made the assumption that maintaining a quiet demeanor was preferable in being considered in having good moral culture.

It is amazing what possibilities exist in a little heartbreak and life chaos. Shortly after yet another pretty nasty breakup, the inevitable life question surfaced: "What is this life about?" I began searching for ways to ease the discomfort of the intense sadness I was feeling and ingesting.

Exploring any and all options that would help to alleviate my falling into the repeated pitfalls I so conveniently plunged into time after time, my mind searched with the intent for healing my heart's hurt... It is true the things that we are taught in childhood can act as seeds and bloom in due time becoming ingrained thoughts. I took inventory of what I was doing and what I was not then I started to remember what was told to me during childhood. "Stillness and quiet will allow you to hear God." I thought, "Okay. Maybe I haven't been the most serene person lately. Perhaps I needed to become still and attempt to listen to the voice of direction that may be attempting to speak to me. I didn't have an exact vehicle to allow arrival to my accomplishment; however, I did recall being told very candidly while complaining during my life's struggles: "If you want something you never had, you must do something you've never done before."

That statement prompted me to revisit the concept of stillness and quiet, with additional questions of what meditation consisted of. I posed a question to myself that was answered swiftly by my inner voice: "Isn't practicing stillness and quiet the same as practicing meditation?" But how do you meditate? And is there any religious affiliation with actually starting it?

Shortly after moving to Los Angeles, I began to view LA as a spiritual mecca. Everywhere you turned, there were different avenues being offered to obtain self-actualization through non-traditional ways. Much different than my experience growing up in Detroit, my spiritual experience was limited and primarily sought after by way of religious participation. Christianity and Islam were the mainstream avenues that I had become familiar with, whether it be Catholic, Baptist, Pentecostal, Adventist, Shiite or Sunni. Outside of attending a local church service in the neighborhood, I was not exposed to many philosophies or practices that enabled me a greater understanding of who I was or the understanding of what it meant to find my purpose; however, I always felt that there existed a dimension of spiritual understanding I had not yet tapped into.

While deciding what method of meditation I wanted to pursue, I encountered one that had no religious affiliation, yet it had a rich history that extended back to India over thousands of years.

I was desperate to begin immediately, hoping that this newfound practice would offer me some peace and clarity that I could layer with the other discoveries I had somehow made.

My questions of what, how, and why regarding meditation would soon be answered when I discovered and attended an information session that was hosted by a local meditation teacher in Venice, California.

This teacher gleamed with light and possessed an insurmountable amount of knowledge concerning consciousness and life principles that impacted our world as people. Words like charm, consciousness, bliss, and transcendence drew me in like a moth to a fire. As the discussion continued, I felt a strange sense of unknown familiarity and reassurance that this practice would provide me with the missing pieces of life I had been seeking.

All attendees of this informational session were provided an overview of the practice and how it worked. It was recommended that meditation be performed twice daily at twenty-minute intervals, once upon waking up and once in the afternoon.

This simple practice was said to provide mental clarity, reduction of stress, promotion of creativity, and increase intellectual ability.

Self-doubt decided to show up. "There is no way you can receive so much for doing so little." I soon would discover that my thoughts were wrong and that learning to go inward for short allotments of time would prove to be one of the greatest investments I had made in myself.

The act of meditating twice daily became second nature, and, while I sometimes experienced an array of challenging thoughts during my practice, the effects outside of meditation in everyday life were incredible and worth every thought endured.

I suddenly felt a shift of more understanding in my everyday awareness and a peace during uncertain chaotic times. The subject of evolution had never meant much to me outside of discussing Darwin's theory in science class; however I had now been opened to understanding the evolving human consciousness, a change for the better. My thought processes sparked with curiosity of positive new interests that previously had been of no interest of. A thirst for understanding the unknown became my focus and priority.

I had lived my whole life attempting to gain consciousness even when I was ignorant of what I was searching for. Meditation provided me with the ability to obtain the answers to the many questions that were present in my life. Here again, the inner being was shown to be the correct force for navigating a well understood life.

The subtle feelings that would influence me during times of decision making became more distinct and less elusive. I made choices about day-to-day life instances without hesitation and also accepted my life experiences without judgment. As time continued with consistent meditation, I viewed life without mistakes, only possibilities to become better.

Perspectives changed when I reflected on past interactions, clarity, and meaning were brought into view. The intention of others that impacted my life experience was brought into the light of full understanding by simply allowing my brain to rest regularly.

Reflecting on the hardships that initiated my search began to have new meaning. The questions I had previously asked myself in journal entries were answered. Why did I judge myself by someone else's standard all these years? My childhood was filled with inconsistencies that did not allow my core value to develop. The need for a positive male influence was absent. I was given love in my childhood however it was without the fundamentals to create productive relationships. My not having these core factors twisted and limited my sense of self.

There are different factors for everyone that influence our potential to suffer. What impacted my emotional misunderstanding may not be the same for you. That does not matter. The solution is universal for everyone: understanding self. No matter how difficult the question or how impactful the trauma endured, daily meditation provides the insight to understand, cope, and thrive during our life experiences.

Avoiding undesired outcomes in situations can require that close observation and details not be overlooked.

Performing meditation gave me the enhanced ability not to overlook what I usually would have during many life situations.

My overreaction of emotions like depression, sadness, and anger that once followed me after a disappointing event, no longer existed. I saw these endings as a sign to renew and initiate something even better.

The very simple practice of shutting my eyes for twenty minutes twice a day had somehow allowed my brain to unite with my spirit within. My instincts became more engaged and more powerful. I gained control over the reactive emotions that so often would dictate my state of being and my interpersonal interactions.

I learned that the best way to answer questions and create satisfaction did not depend on the media, a man or my peers. My ongoing commitment to myself proves that I am the greatest authority for my life.

(Journal entry)

Loving ourselves can sometimes appear to be more difficult than one would expect. Accept the many changes that come while growing and embracing practices that can enhance our development. Life is an ongoing process of discovery.

Life is filled with unpredictable events. They are both joyous and disappointing. However our inner self determines how we process the emotions that come along with various circumstances.

I am a firm believer that we never stop growing or learning unless we want a life without purpose. My journey to find sustainable tools for emotional wellness was complete. The act of performing self-evaluating activities, affirming my desires, and resting my brain gave me the perfect combination for pressing forward and living a life I so desired to lead.

Meditation
Step 3 of Your Path to Egypt

In the midst of movement and chaos, keep stillness inside of you.
~Deepak Chopra

Meditation is the act of sitting quietly with eyes closed for a period of time. (Twenty minutes is recommended for optimal experience.) It is a mental exercise that requires you to disconnect from the exterior stimulus and focus on your breath, a chosen mantra, or affirmation.

People choose from a variety of methods. For beginning meditators, I recommend breath meditation, taking notice of your inhalations and exhalations. Everyone breaths; it is a natural automatic function and the easiest to start with.

The key is to have eyes closed and an intended desire of going within, allowing any thoughts that arise to be experienced and acknowledged. The act of meditating allows all unconscious aspects of our inner self to emerge and be validated. It allows your higher self to emerge because we are ridding any distractions by closing our eyes in silence.

Meditation is not a new phenomenon; it has been around and practiced for ages throughout history. Meditation does not dictate your religious belief or affiliation, only a vehicle of allowing a connection with your higher power or self.

Instructions for starting

- Identify a twenty-minute block of time before you begin your day.
- Insure there are no radios or televisions turned on to decrease any distraction.
- Sit in an upright comfortable position.
- Set an intention of what you want to achieve for the day.
- Choose a subtle alarm to give you notice that twenty minutes has elapsed. (A phone alarm is fine.)
- Close your eyes and focus on your breathing, taking normal breathes focus on inhalations and exhalations.

During your meditation, you will experience a wide array of thoughts from prevalent thoughts about your life to thoughts you may feel have no relevance. The purpose is to allow whatever thoughts that come up be acknowledged. All thoughts that arise during meditation may not be pleasant or enjoyable; however, you must remember that the benefit of meditation happens during daily life not necessarily during your practice.

Regular meditation practice shifts our awareness. We become more in tune with our individual purpose, strengths, and coping. The buildup of life stress is released each time we go silent and shut down exterior stimuli, allowing our brains to rest and our inner self to adequately connect.

Maintaining a daily schedule of meditation will give you the tools needed to be successful and overcome any trauma that you have experienced. It provides the needed emotional rest to recognize better paths with life choices and the ability to recognize subtleties otherwise overlooked. It does not seem foreign to give our bodies a needed rest if we are running or doing strenuous physical activity, so the idea of giving our brain the same consideration only enhances its function, just as rest enhances the function of the body.

Engaging in meditation before you begin your day and after its complete creates the best mental clarity for our minds. It allows us to move forward without emotional fatigue because every thought that comes about has the need to be experienced and acknowledged. Our meditation practice allows those thoughts to do exactly that: freeing up space mentally and providing needed energy to move forward with productive goal attainment.

Being vigilant about our emotional wellness is the only way of creating better lives and overcoming hurdles that we had to jump. Most women are okay with performing exercises that change our exterior appearance, whether it be to diet for loss of weight, apply makeup to enhance our facial features, and even shopping for clothing that accentuates our bodies, but what about our emotional health? Many of us fail to maintain a commitment to enhance our inner beauty and ability to maintain happiness from within. Performing the self-care activities I've discussed will do exactly that. I am a living witness.

"I have aborted so many pregnancies believing that it was the right thing to do for the sake of convenience. I was so wrong and I didn't understand the mystery of life until I held my child Faith something suddenly hit me to let me know she was really mine. I also realized I needed no one but my child to make my life complete. So everything that I fought, cried and prayed for wasn't even necessary—'the relationship with someone forbidden.'

"I have scarred myself sexually, emotionally and physically for the sake of so-called love. It's so sad my soul and mind have been compromised for nothing. No one deserves the abuse I've endured for anything especially a man. I need to forgive myself for my mistakes and understand that is all they are: mistakes."

Each time I read this above journal entry, I cannot help but say, "Thank You, God!" I was allotted grace after enduring such a high level of trauma. I can clearly remember the intense hurt and desperation I felt when writing those thoughts after I had suffered a stillborn birth. It awoke desperation with determination in the same breathe.

At that time, I was the unhealthiest emotionally and mentally I have ever been in my life. I was holding on to a destructive relationship, intensely grieving the loss of my child and trying to come to grips with the guilt of terminating past pregnancies. Is this why my baby did not live? I do not deserve to be a mother. After all, I did not choose to continue my previous pregnancies (none of that was true.) However, it was the thoughts that constantly bombarded my mind daily. Intense sadness compelled my body after the loss. I tried focusing on a goal to make myself relevant and continued to pursue my nursing education. I was stretching myself like a rubber band and was emotionally fatigued, but the memory of holding my baby fueled my desire to press forward.

It was difficult since the one person I knew would love me unconditionally left this world the same day she entered it.

My thoughts on motherhood really became conflicted after the loss. Unconsciously, I felt I did not deserve the precious gift of being a mom, and, secondly, I doubted my ability to raise a healthy, happy child since I had not done the best job protecting myself. The choices that I had made were self-destructive and certainly did not make for a productive life. How was I going to provide the essentials for a good outcome if I had not done it for myself?

The lights came on when I held my sweet gift in my arms and the vehicle of healing was granted.

I could not have imagined at that time when I suffered such a great loss that I would someday be emotionally sound and be granted another opportunity to become a mother. My emotional investment paid off. I entered a healthy relationship established in love, compassion, and acceptance. My choice of past relationships was built on control, illusions of a missing father, and an inability to value my core self. The falsities I once embraced as truth were now a thing of the past.

In 2019, I was immensely blessed with the opportunity to birth another daughter, Egypt Nile. She was healthy, perfect, full of life, and the love that I had contemplated for so long. The trials and life lessons leading up to the day I birthed her had all been worth it!

It was hard to imagine that, years later, my arms were again filled with another beautiful soul, only this time, I was emotionally whole and she was full of life. I was not told to say goodbye. She was mine and here to stay for the duration. I was more than equipped to offer to her the love she deserved and embrace the motherhood I desired.

The journey to Egypt was not expeditious or easy, but my arrival was to a place of most high! What a gratifying climb up the pyramid.

An unexplainable, unimaginable love was granted unto me and a realization that I had been worthy and capable of love all along. I unknowingly possessed within everything I needed for a life filled with love and acceptance. The self-work I engaged in over the years allowed my life circumstances, perspective, and, most importantly, my emotional wellbeing to be elevated. Like many of us, I was never given specific instructions for coping with hardships and how to recover from trauma, but, with my life research and identifying key strategies, I discovered a trilogy that has assisted many women in turning their hurt into wellness.

> *Consciousness was all I ever needed even during the times I was ignorant of what it was I desired.*
>
> ~ Kenya Lee

Today I am a wife, mother, registered nurse, educator, and advocate for any woman with the desire the journey to emotional wellness, despite whatever negative life challenges she's come against. I engage in daily meditation, practicing daily affirmations of my desires and journaling daily. These practical tools provide me with the ability to continually reach the life goals I have set for myself. Aside from motherhood my self-discovery has been my greatest accomplishment. Every question I posed to myself in the displayed journal entries have been answered with clarity and truth. They were all answered by me and the wisdom that emerged when I searched within. The Trinity Strategy is a powerful and proven method to overcome trauma and to evolve abundantly.

I persevered to my desired destination in life despite facing many challenging life circumstances and self-limiting behaviors. The change of my emotional outlook led me to a place I feel proud to call my own.

My outlook on happiness is not complex. It involves taking whatever obstacles we are faced with and changing them to our desired outcome. Implementing the Trinity Strategy(three daily practices) provided me the opportunity to evolve into my full potential and will allow you to evolve into yours.

My path to Egypt, a land that is both defined as a place of bondage and refuge proved to be my place of refuge. Refuge from self-limiting behaviors, refuge from low self-esteem and refuge from negativity. It is the place where my healing, growth and transformation took place. It is where I continue to elevate.

My understanding of my self-value gives me unlimited ability to achieve, succeed and thrive in whatever capacity is necessary. Performing the Trinity Strategy discussed in this book doesn't stop life circumstances from happening but it does grant the ability to cope and remain in a place of emotional wellness.

Wherever you choose to go in your life is entirely up to you. No one else has the power to dictate your destination. The travel itinerary is entirely yours to design.

A Thirty-Day Plan for Daily Check-in Morning & Evening

The use of the Trinity Strategy described earlier will create a shift in your emotional awareness in just 30days. Challenge yourself to start the daily activities of Journaling, Affirming and Meditation. Evaluate your progress after one month and experience a huge increase of clarity and the direction to reach your desired goals.

> *I wake up every morning and tell myself*
> *"Good morning gorgeous"*
> *Sometimes you gotta look in the mirror and say*
> *"Good morning gorgeous"*
>
> ~Mary J Blige. *"Good Morning Gorgeous"*

DATE: _____

MORNING CHECK IN   ☐

I am feeling _____

I am grateful for _____

Meditation   ☐

Today's Affirmation: _____

_____

Journal: _____

_____

_____

_____

_____

EVENING CHECK IN ☐

I am grateful for_____

I am feeling_____

Meditation ☐

What was the best part of my day today:

_____

_____

What goals did I achieve? _____

_____

What makes my life special? _____

_____

_____

> *And if at first you don't succeed, the dust yourself off and try again.*
>
> ~ Aaliyah *"Try Again"*

DATE: _____

MORNING CHECK IN ☐

I am feeling _____

I am grateful for_____

Meditation ☐

Today's Affirmation: _____
_____

Journal: _____
_____
_____
_____
_____
_____

EVENING CHECK IN ☐

I am grateful for_____

I am feeling_____

Meditation ☐

What was the best part of my day today:

_____

_____

What goals did I achieve? _____

_____

What makes my life special? _____

_____

_____

> *In the middle of difficulty lies opportunity.*
> ~ Albert Einstein

DATE: _____

MORNING CHECK IN ☐

I am feeling _____

I am grateful for _____

Meditation ☐

Today's Affirmation: _____

_____

Journal: _____

_____

_____

_____

_____

_____

EVENING CHECK IN ☐

I am grateful for_____

I am feeling_____

Meditation ☐

What was the best part of my day today:

_____

_____

What goals did I achieve? _____

_____

What makes my life special? _____

_____

_____

> *This is a beautiful day, I've never seen this one before.*
>
> ~ Maya Angelou

DATE: _____

MORNING CHECK IN ☐

I am feeling _____

I am grateful for _____

Meditation ☐

Today's Affirmation: _____

_____

Journal: _____

_____

_____

_____

_____

_____

EVENING CHECK IN ☐

I am grateful for_____

I am feeling_____

Meditation ☐

What was the best part of my day today:

_____

_____

What goals did I achieve? _____

_____

What makes my life special? _____

_____

_____

> *But just because it burns, doesn't mean you're gonna die. You gotta get up and try, and try, and try.*
>
> ~ Pink, *"Try"*

DATE: _____

MORNING CHECK IN ☐

I am feeling _____

I am grateful for _____

Meditation ☐

Today's Affirmation: _____

_____

Journal: _____

_____

_____

_____

_____

_____

EVENING CHECK IN ☐

I am grateful for_____

I am feeling_____

Meditation ☐

What was the best part of my day today:

_____

_____

What goals did I achieve? _____

_____

What makes my life special? _____

_____

_____

> *Change is inevitable. Why hold onto what you have to let go of?*
>
> ~ Jhene Aiko

DATE: _____

MORNING CHECK IN ☐

I am feeling _____

I am grateful for_____

Meditation ☐

Today's Affirmation: _____

_____

Journal: _____

_____

_____

_____

_____

_____

EVENING CHECK IN □

I am grateful for_____

I am feeling_____

Meditation □

What was the best part of my day today:

_____

_____

What goals did I achieve? _____

_____

What makes my life special? _____

_____

_____

> *Death is not the greatest loss in life. The greatest loss is what dies inside while still alive. Never surrender.*
>
> ~ Tupac Shakur

DATE: _____

MORNING CHECK IN ☐

I am feeling _____

I am grateful for _____

Meditation ☐

Today's Affirmation: _____

_____

Journal: _____

_____

_____

_____

_____

_____

_____

EVENING CHECK IN ☐

I am grateful for_____

I am feeling_____

Meditation ☐

What was the best part of my day today:

_____

_____

What goals did I achieve? _____

_____

What makes my life special? _____

_____

_____

> *I have a greater purpose. God put something in my heart to get across and that's what I'm going to focus on, using my voice as an instrument and doing what needs to be done.*
>
> ~ Kendrick Lamar

DATE: _____

MORNING CHECK IN ☐

I am feeling _____

I am grateful for _____

Meditation ☐

Today's Affirmation: _____

_____

Journal: _____

_____

_____

_____

EVENING CHECK IN ☐

I am grateful for_____

I am feeling_____

Meditation ☐

What was the best part of my day today:

_____

_____

What goals did I achieve? _____

_____

What makes my life special? _____

_____

_____

> *I keep my head high, I got my wings to carry me. I don't know freedom, I want my dreams to rescue me.*
>
> ~ J Cole

DATE: _____

MORNING CHECK IN ☐

I am feeling _____

I am grateful for_____

Meditation ☐

Today's Affirmation: _____

_____

Journal: _____

_____

_____

_____

_____

_____

_____

EVENING CHECK IN ☐

I am grateful for_____

I am feeling_____

Meditation ☐

What was the best part of my day today:

_____

_____

What goals did I achieve? _____

_____

What makes my life special? _____

_____

_____

> *Most important thing is to get rid of doubt.*
> *If you got doubt in what you're doing it's*
> *not gonna work.*
>
> ~ Nipsey Hussle

DATE: _____

MORNING CHECK IN ☐

I am feeling _____

I am grateful for _____

Meditation ☐

Today's Affirmation: _____

_____

Journal: _____

_____

_____

_____

_____

_____

EVENING CHECK IN ☐

I am grateful for_____

I am feeling_____

Meditation ☐

What was the best part of my day today:

_____

_____

What goals did I achieve? _____

_____

What makes my life special? _____

_____

_____

> *When you undervalue what you do the world will undervalue who you are.*
>
> ~ Oprah Winfrey

DATE: _____

MORNING CHECK IN ☐

I am feeling _____

I am grateful for_____

Meditation ☐

Today's Affirmation: _____

_____

Journal: _____

_____

_____

_____

_____

_____

EVENING CHECK IN ☐

I am grateful for_____

I am feeling_____

Meditation ☐

What was the best part of my day today:

_____

_____

What goals did I achieve? _____

_____

What makes my life special? _____

_____

_____

> *Your life is yours to live, no matter how you choose to live it. When you do not think about how you intend to live it, it lives you. When you occupy it, step into it consciously, you live it.*
>
> ~ Gary Zukav

DATE: _____

MORNING CHECK IN   ☐

I am feeling _____

I am grateful for _____

Meditation   ☐

Today's Affirmation: _____

_____

Journal: _____

_____

_____

_____

EVENING CHECK IN ☐

I am grateful for_____

I am feeling_____

Meditation ☐

What was the best part of my day today:

_____

_____

What goals did I achieve? _____

_____

What makes my life special? _____

_____

_____

> *There is nothing stronger than a broken woman who has rebuilt herself.*
>
> ~ Hannah Gadsby

DATE: _____

MORNING CHECK IN ☐

I am feeling _____

I am grateful for _____

Meditation ☐

Today's Affirmation: _____

_____

Journal: _____

_____

_____

_____

_____

_____

EVENING CHECK IN ☐

I am grateful for_____

I am feeling_____

Meditation ☐

What was the best part of my day today:

_____

_____

What goals did I achieve? _____

_____

What makes my life special? _____

_____

_____

> You and I possess within ourselves at every moment of our lives, under all circumstances, the power to transform the quality of our lives.
>
> ~ Werner Erhard

DATE: _____

MORNING CHECK IN ☐

I am feeling _____

I am grateful for _____

Meditation ☐

Today's Affirmation: _____

_____

Journal: _____

_____

_____

_____

EVENING CHECK IN ☐

I am grateful for_____

I am feeling_____

Meditation ☐

What was the best part of my day today:

_____

_____

What goals did I achieve? _____

_____

What makes my life special? _____

_____

_____

Yesterday I was clever so I wanted to change the world. Today I am wise so I am changing myself.

~ Rumi

DATE: _____

MORNING CHECK IN ☐

I am feeling _____

I am grateful for_____

Meditation ☐

Today's Affirmation: _____

_____

Journal: _____

_____

_____

_____

_____

_____

EVENING CHECK IN ☐

I am grateful for_____

I am feeling_____

Meditation ☐

What was the best part of my day today:

_____

_____

What goals did I achieve? _____

_____

What makes my life special? _____

_____

_____

> *There's nowhere you can be that isn't where you're meant to be.*
>
> ~ John Lennon

DATE: _____

MORNING CHECK IN   ☐

I am feeling _____

I am grateful for_____

Meditation   ☐

Today's Affirmation: _____

_____

Journal: _____

_____

_____

_____

_____

_____

EVENING CHECK IN ☐

I am grateful for_____

I am feeling_____

Meditation ☐

What was the best part of my day today:

_____

_____

What goals did I achieve? _____

_____

What makes my life special? _____

_____

_____

> *Transformation isn't a future event, it's a*
> *present day activity.*
>
> ~ Jilian Michaels

DATE: _____

MORNING CHECK IN ☐

I am feeling _____

I am grateful for_____

Meditation ☐

Today's Affirmation: _____

_____

Journal: _____

_____

_____

_____

_____

_____

EVENING CHECK IN ☐

I am grateful for_____

I am feeling_____

Meditation ☐

What was the best part of my day today:

_____

_____

What goals did I achieve? _____

_____

What makes my life special? _____

_____

_____

> *Nothing happens until the pain of remaining the same outweighs the pain of change.*
>
> ~ Arthur Burt

DATE: _____

MORNING CHECK IN ☐

I am feeling _____

I am grateful for_____

Meditation ☐

Today's Affirmation: _____

_____

Journal: _____

_____

_____

_____

_____

_____

_____

EVENING CHECK IN ☐

I am grateful for _____

I am feeling _____

Meditation ☐

What was the best part of my day today:

_____

_____

What goals did I achieve? _____

_____

What makes my life special? _____

_____

_____

We delight in the beauty of the butterfly, but rarely admit the changes it has gone through to achieve that beauty.

~ Maya Angelou

DATE: _____

MORNING CHECK IN ☐

I am feeling _____

I am grateful for_____

Meditation ☐

Today's Affirmation: _____

_____

Journal: _____

_____

_____

_____

_____

_____

EVENING CHECK IN ☐

I am grateful for_____

I am feeling_____

Meditation ☐

What was the best part of my day today:

_____

_____

What goals did I achieve? _____

_____

What makes my life special? _____

_____

_____

> *Everything in the universe is within you.*
> *Ask all from yourself.*
>
> ~ Rumi

DATE: _____

MORNING CHECK IN   ☐

I am feeling _____

I am grateful for_____

Meditation   ☐

Today's Affirmation: _____
_____

Journal: _____
_____
_____
_____
_____
_____

EVENING CHECK IN ☐

I am grateful for_____

I am feeling_____

Meditation ☐

What was the best part of my day today:

_____

_____

What goals did I achieve? _____

_____

What makes my life special? _____

_____

_____

> *What counts can't always be counted; what can be counted doesn't always count.*
>
> ~ Albert Einstein

DATE: _____

MORNING CHECK IN   ☐

I am feeling _____

I am grateful for_____

Meditation   ☐

Today's Affirmation: _____

_____

Journal: _____

_____

_____

_____

_____

_____

_____

EVENING CHECK IN ☐

I am grateful for_____

I am feeling_____

Meditation ☐

What was the best part of my day today:

_____

_____

What goals did I achieve? _____

_____

What makes my life special? _____

_____

_____

> *We delight in the beauty of the butterfly,*
> *but rarely admit the changes it has gone*
> *through to achieve that beauty.*
>
> ~ Maya Angelou

DATE: _____

MORNING CHECK IN   ☐

I am feeling _____

I am grateful for _____

Meditation   ☐

Today's Affirmation: _____

_____

Journal: _____

_____

_____

_____

_____

_____

EVENING CHECK IN ☐

I am grateful for_____

I am feeling_____

Meditation ☐

What was the best part of my day today:

_____

_____

What goals did I achieve? _____

_____

What makes my life special? _____

_____

_____

The more you praise and celebrate your life, the more there is in life to celebrate..

~ Oprah Winfrey

DATE: _____

MORNING CHECK IN ☐

I am feeling _____

I am grateful for _____

Meditation ☐

Today's Affirmation: _____

_____

Journal: _____

_____

_____

_____

_____

_____

_____

EVENING CHECK IN ☐

I am grateful for_____

I am feeling_____

Meditation ☐

What was the best part of my day today:

_____

_____

What goals did I achieve? _____

_____

What makes my life special? _____

_____

_____

> *If you don't love yourself, you cannot love others.*
>
> ~ Dalai Lama

DATE: _____

MORNING CHECK IN ☐

I am feeling _____

I am grateful for_____

Meditation ☐

Today's Affirmation: _____

_____

Journal: _____

_____

_____

_____

_____

_____

EVENING CHECK IN ☐

I am grateful for_____

I am feeling_____

Meditation ☐

What was the best part of my day today:

_____

_____

What goals did I achieve? _____

_____

What makes my life special? _____

_____

_____

> *Acknowledging the good that you already have in your life is the foundation for all abundance.*
>
> ~ Eckart Tolle

DATE: _____

MORNING CHECK IN ☐

I am feeling _____

I am grateful for_____

Meditation ☐

Today's Affirmation: _____

_____

Journal: _____

_____

_____

_____

_____

_____

EVENING CHECK IN ☐

I am grateful for_____

I am feeling_____

Meditation ☐

What was the best part of my day today:

_____

_____

What goals did I achieve? _____

_____

What makes my life special? _____

_____

_____

> *Success is only meaningful and enjoyable if it feels like your own.*
>
> ~ Michelle Obama

DATE: _____

MORNING CHECK IN ☐

I am feeling _____

I am grateful for _____

Meditation ☐

Today's Affirmation: _____

_____

Journal: _____

_____

_____

_____

_____

_____

EVENING CHECK IN ☐

I am grateful for_____

I am feeling_____

Meditation ☐

What was the best part of my day today:

_____

_____

What goals did I achieve? _____

_____

What makes my life special? _____

_____

_____

> *The most alluring thing a woman can have is confidence.*
>
> ~ Beyonce

DATE: _____

MORNING CHECK IN ☐

I am feeling _____

I am grateful for _____

Meditation ☐

Today's Affirmation: _____

_____

Journal: _____

_____

_____

_____

_____

_____

EVENING CHECK IN ☐

I am grateful for_____

I am feeling_____

Meditation ☐

What was the best part of my day today:

_____

_____

What goals did I achieve? _____

_____

What makes my life special? _____

_____

_____

> *Everything you want to be, you already are. You're simply on the path to discovering it.*

DATE: _____

MORNING CHECK IN ☐

I am feeling _____

I am grateful for_____

Meditation ☐

Today's Affirmation: _____

_____

Journal: _____

_____

_____

_____

_____

_____

EVENING CHECK IN ☐

I am grateful for_____

I am feeling_____

Meditation ☐

What was the best part of my day today:

_____

_____

What goals did I achieve? _____

_____

What makes my life special? _____

_____

_____

Comparison is an act of violence against the self.

~ Iyanla Vanzant

DATE: _____

MORNING CHECK IN ☐

I am feeling _____

I am grateful for _____

Meditation ☐

Today's Affirmation: _____

_____

Journal: _____

_____

_____

_____

_____

_____

EVENING CHECK IN ☐

I am grateful for_____

I am feeling_____

Meditation ☐

What was the best part of my day today:

_____

_____

What goals did I achieve? _____

_____

What makes my life special? _____

_____

_____

> *A strong woman knows she has strength enough for the journey, but a woman of strength knows it is in the journey where she will become strong.*
>
> ~ Unknown

DATE: _____

MORNING CHECK IN ☐

I am feeling _____

I am grateful for_____

Meditation ☐

Today's Affirmation: _____

_____

Journal: _____

_____

_____

_____

_____

EVENING CHECK IN   ☐

I am grateful for_____

I am feeling_____

Meditation   ☐

What was the best part of my day today:

_____

_____

What goals did I achieve? _____

_____

What makes my life special? _____

_____

_____

www.ingramcontent.com/pod-product-compliance
Lightning Source LLC
Chambersburg PA
CBHW051627120626
46551CB00014B/1966